Lin, Sam, an Jake

16

Written by Nina Muñoz

Illustrated by Alex Robinson

Short *a* (CVC words)		Long *a* (VCe words)	
cap		cape	made
mad		grade	make
Sam		Jake	same

High-Frequency Words

are	give	little
away	like	they

1

See Lin, Sam, and Jake.
They are in the same grade.

Lin and Sam go away.

Jake gets a little mad.

Lin and Sam make gifts.
They like to give gifts to Jake.

Lin made a cap for Jake.
Sam made a cape for Jake.

Lin and Sam give the gifts to Jake.

Jake likes his gifts.